Con

Say the Sounds	4
Tricky Words	5
Meet the Characters	6
The Tree That Blinked	7
What's in the Box?	25
The Old Red Tractor	43
The Model Boat	61
Wait and See!	79
The Bad-Tempered Goat	97
Book Review	116
Character Review	118

This book belongs to

Meet the Characters

- Bee
- Rags
- Inky
- Farmer Green
- Zack
- Ben
- Jess
- Snake
- Sally
- Tolly
- Neb
- Phonic
- Gramps
- Molly

The Tree That Blinked

Inky, Snake and Bee went to the forest. They took Phonic with them on the laptop and set him up in a glade. Then they went off to look for chestnuts.

They liked chestnuts and were going to roast them on a pan in the fire when they got home. They had made a pile of chestnuts next to Phonic.

Snake slithered up the trees and knocked the chestnuts down to Inky and Bee, who cracked the prickly shells and collected the nuts.

One of the chestnuts fell under a tree, and Bee rushed off to fetch it.

"Got you!" said Bee, grabbing the chestnut. She picked it up and stood up. Then, as she looked at the tree, it seemed that the tree looked back at her. "Help!" buzzed Bee in alarm.

Help!

Bee fled back to Inky, Phonic and Snake.
 "Help!" she cried again. "That tree was looking at me."
Snake, Inky and Phonic looked at Bee.
 "I think she must have had too much sun," hissed Snake, and shook his head.

"It did," buzzed Bee. "That tree looked at me."

"Do not be silly, Bee," hissed Snake. "Trees cannot look at you."

"Well, this one did," insisted Bee. "Come and see."

Inky picked up Phonic, and Bee led them to the tree.

"There," she said, pointing to it. The tree looked at them and then blinked. "See," whispered Bee. "It *is* looking at us."

"No," said Phonic. "Look, there is a hole in the tree and there is something in the hole."

Snake slithered up and looked inside the hole. He found himself looking at someone who was hanging upside down.

"It looks like a mouse with wings!" called Snake.

"A mouse with wings?" said Inky. "There is no such thing!"

Snake looked into the hole a second time.

"Yup," he said. "It still looks like a mouse with wings to me."

"I think it is you who has had too much sun," said Bee.

"Hmm... a mouse with wings..." mused Phonic. "I think you can see a bat."

"A bat?" said Snake, looking into the hole again. "Yes," he agreed, "I think it *is* a bat."

Just then, the bat shot out of his hole and Snake ducked, lost his grip and fell off the tree.

Ouch!

"Ouch!" yelled Snake as he hit the ground.

The bat hung upside down at the top of the tree, blinking in the sunshine.

"Come back!" Inky shouted up to him. "We will not harm you!"

The bat blinked and then explained, "I was afraid! All the noise woke me up and then, when I looked out, there was a big snake looking in at me."

"Yes, there was," admitted Inky, "but he will not harm you," she added quickly, seeing the bat start to unwrap his wings again.

"Sorry," said Snake. "We were collecting chestnuts. I just looked in to see who was there."

"It is just my family and me," said the bat. "In winter we sleep in a cave and in summer we live in a big loft. But when we came back this summer, our home was gone. It had been converted into a room.

We have been living in this tree while we look for somewhere else to live."

"Well," said Phonic, "perhaps we can help. We need to think of somewhere dark that is not too noisy and that has plenty of room for bats to roost in."

"Roast in?" said Bee. "Roast in? Is that a joke, Phonic?"

"No, Bee," Phonic explained. "*Roost* in, not roast in. When bats are hanging upside down and sleeping, it is called roosting."

"What about the shed?" said Bee.

"No, it is too small," objected Snake.

"There is no room for the bats to hang upside down there," agreed Inky.

"I think," said Phonic, "that I have just the spot. Come on, Inky, you will have to help me."

They set off, Inky carrying Phonic, then Snake, Bee and the bat. They stopped when they came to the farm.

"There," said Phonic. "What about the big old stone barn? There is plenty of room, it is dark, and there are lots of holes the bats can use for going in and out."

"Perfect!" said the bat, happily. "I must go and tell my family."

"And we can go home and roast our chestnuts," said Bee. "No more trees that blink for me!"

What's in the book?

What are Inky, Snake and Bee going to do with the chestnuts?
What does Bee tell Inky and Snake about the tree?
Why were the bats living in the tree?

What do you think?

Why is Bee scared of the tree?
How did the bats feel when they lost their home?

What's in the Box?

One morning, Inky, Snake and Bee had seen such a lot of cartoons that they were getting restless.

"I am bored," said Snake, stretching. "Let's do something else."

"Like what?" said Inky and Bee, looking up.

Snake shrugged.

"What about hide and seek?" he said.

"No," said Inky and Bee. "You win every time!"

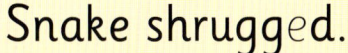

"What about Monopoly?" said Inky.

"No," said Snake. "I am sick of sitting down."

"What about a game of 'What's in the box?'" said Phonic, from his corner.

Inky, Bee and Snake listened while Phonic explained the rules. "You have a box," he said, "and you go and collect things to fill it with. All the things must fit in the box. Then we see what everyone has found."

Sounds fun!

"I like the sound of that!" said Snake, and Inky and Bee agreed with him. So Inky found three empty boxes and off they all went. Inky and Snake rushed off to the shed and Bee zoomed outside, where she buzzed around in a panic.

"What will go into my box? What will go into my box?" she kept buzzing.

Back at the mouse hole, Phonic found himself alone.

"What can I do while I am waiting?" he brooded. Then he smiled. His screen went blank and then filled up with lots of little green and red ships, which floated across it. Phonic liked this game!

"Bip, bip, ping... kersplat!" A little green ship went up in flames.

"Got you!" muttered Phonic.

Outside, Inky looked around. Then she looked down at her box. It seemed very small indeed. She looked around again.
 "Perfect!" she exclaimed as she picked something off the ground.

Just then, Bee zipped by.
 "What shall I get? What shall I get?" she was still buzzing, frantically.

Snake was looking around too. He scratched his head.

"Perfect!" he exclaimed, picking something up.

Just then, Bee whizzed by again.

"What will fit? What will fit?" she buzzed.

Snake slithered back to the shed.

"There must be something in here that will fit in my box," he hissed. "Yesss!" he hissed happily, picking up something else and slipping it into his box.

Just then, Bee rushed by again.

"What shall I get? What shall I get?" she buzzed.

Inky was still in the garden. She tried looking under a tree, where she soon found something. She picked it up and tucked it into her box.

"Good," she said to herself. "Where shall I go next?"

Good!

Just then, Bee came speeding by.

"What will fit? What shall I get?" she buzzed.

Bee was still frantically hunting for things to go in her box.

"Help!" she was muttering, when suddenly she spotted a feather. "Yes!" she exclaimed. "That will just fit in my box."

A feather!

She swooped down to pick the feather up.

Inky shut her box.

"That's it!" she said. "I have finished." She looked around. Snake was sitting next to his box, sunning himself. "Have you finished?" called Inky.

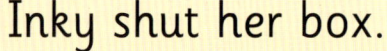

Finished!

Me too!

"Yes," said Snake, sitting up. They looked around.

"Where is Bee?" said Inky. They looked and looked but Bee was nowhere about.

"Where can she be?" said Snake. He and Inky looked everywhere, but Bee was still nowhere to be found. "Perhaps she has finished too," said Snake. "Let's see if she is back with Phonic."

Back at the mouse hole, they found Bee's box on the desk, but Bee herself was not there.

"Phonic!" called Inky.

"Er... here I am," said Phonic, who quickly hid his game and popped back onto the screen.

"Have you seen Bee?" said Snake.

"No, sorry, I was just... er... checking this game," he confessed. "Is that her box there?" Snake and Inky nodded.

"Yes," they agreed, "but we cannot see Bee. We have looked and looked."

"Well, we had better start without her." said Phonic, "but perhaps she will come back soon. She cannot have gone far."

"Come on then," he continued. "Let's see what you collected in your boxes." Inky had found a stamp that someone had dropped by the shed. Next she took out a striped seed, a bit of green string, some sand from the sand box and a small stone with a hole in it.

"Good job, Inky!" cried Snake and Phonic.

Snake started to take the things out of his box. There was a rubber band, a nail from the shed, a twig, some red wool, and a doll's boot that had been dropped on the ground outside.

"Good job, Snake!" exclaimed Inky and Phonic.

They looked around but Bee was still nowhere to be seen.

"Where can she be?" said Inky.

"Well, let's see what she collected," said Phonic.

Inky scampered up to Bee's box. She tried to see what was inside it, but the box was too heavy for her. Snake slithered up to help. Together they slid the top of the box off, and there inside it was Bee, sound asleep on the feather!

"All that buzzing around looking for things must have worn her out," smiled Inky.

What's in the book?

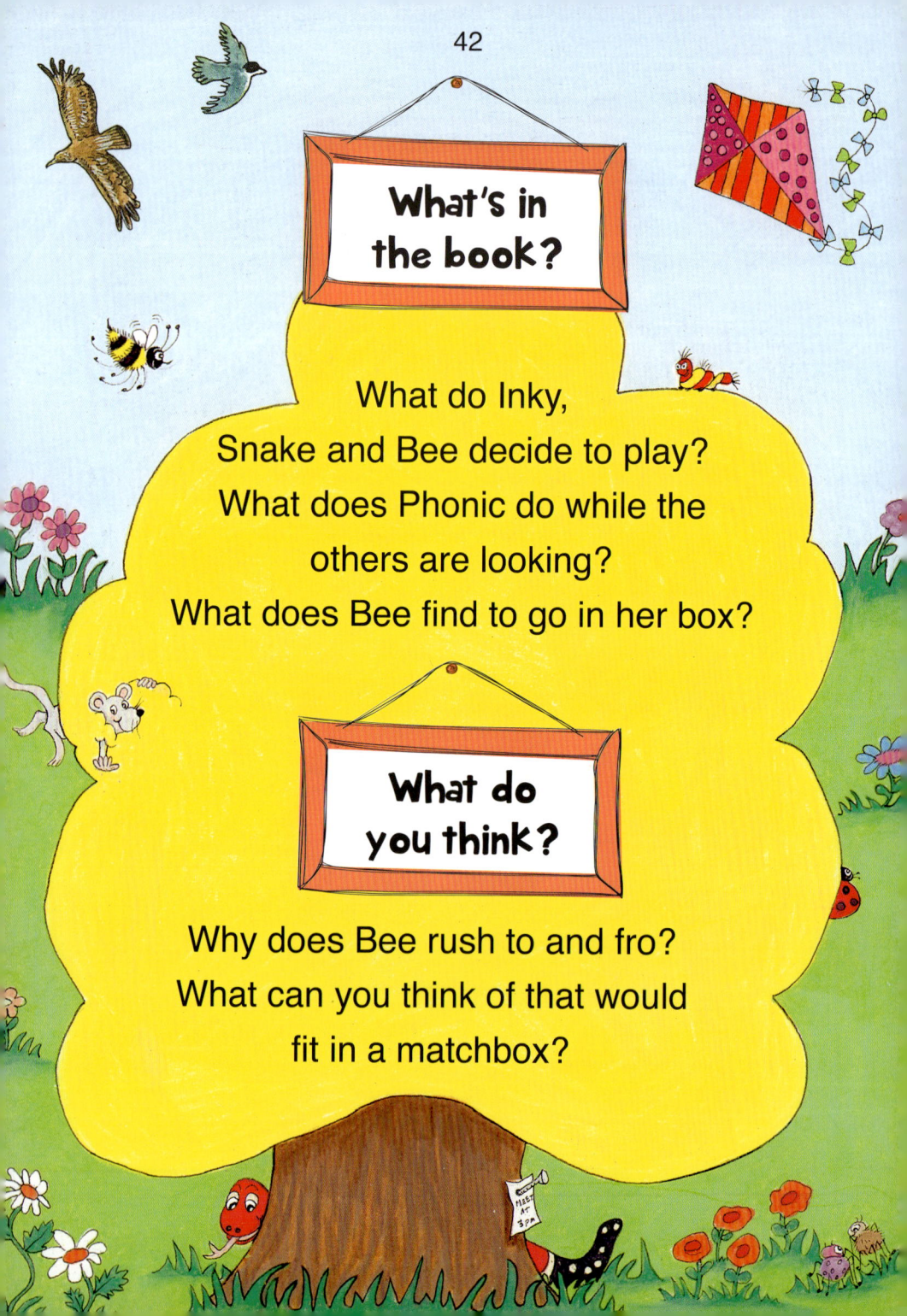

What do Inky, Snake and Bee decide to play?
What does Phonic do while the others are looking?
What does Bee find to go in her box?

What do you think?

Why does Bee rush to and fro?
What can you think of that would fit in a matchbox?

The Old Red Tractor

In a corner of Moat Farm stood an old barn. It was dark in the barn and Farmer Green stored lots of things there, like old horse-carts, tools and bits of wood. Some of these things had been stored there for so long that Farmer Green had forgotten all about them.

On one side of the barn was an old red tractor. It was a little bit rusty and there were cobwebs hanging down from it. Apart from Molly and Tolly, who often slept there, no one came in the barn much.

Zzzz.

One evening, the big green tractor had broken down. Farmer Green was in the yard, mending it. He stood up and scratched his head under his cap.

"It is too late to go and get the part I need," he said to himself. "It will have to wait until morning."

Cluck!

Just then, he happened to look up at the barn.

"Hmm," he said, thinking. "Perhaps, in the barn, there is an old part that I can use to mend the tractor. If there is, I can finish my jobs off this evening, instead of waiting. I need this big tractor to help with the harvest as I can attach the big grain-trailer to it."

Farmer Green went to the barn and looked into the gloom.

In the barn, he found himself standing next to the old red tractor. He looked at it and rubbed its paint.

"You were a good old thing," he said, patting it fondly. "I had forgotten you were in here. Still, I suppose I must get on."

I had forgotten you were here!

He went back to looking for the part he needed to mend the big green tractor. He bent down and picked up some bits of metal from the ground.

"No, no," he muttered, and shook his head. Then he found something under some wood. "That looks more like it!" he said, but when he looked at it properly, he said, "No, this is no good. I need something bigger."

Next, Farmer Green looked around at the back of the barn.

"This looks more promising," he said, as he found a box crammed with old odds and ends. "Yes! Perfect!" he exclaimed, as he stood up. "This will do the job," and off he set to finish mending the big green tractor.

Perfect!

Just as he was about to go outside, Farmer Green stopped and looked back at the old red tractor.

"Hmm!" he said, rubbing his chin. "I need a small tractor to help me. And all this one needs is some oil and a good brush-down."

"Hmm!"

Next morning, he came back to start mending the old red tractor. He took it out of the barn and into the yard, where it stood looking dusty and battered.

A lot of dust!

Farmer Green brushed off all the cobwebs and dust. Then he fetched his hose and scrubbed the tractor down.

He spent the whole weekend mending the tractor.

"Well," said Sally, his wife, when he had finished, "the tractor looks better. Let's see if she drives better, too."

"That's better!"

Farmer Green clambered up into the tractor.

"Fingers crossed!" he called.

The tractor roared into life, and there was a big cloud of smoke. Ben and Neb woke up and started barking loudly. Molly, Tolly and the hens all ran to hide. Farmer Green took the brake off and started to drive the old red tractor around the yard.

When he got back to Sally, she clapped.
"There is going to be an old tractor rally next weekend," she said. "What about entering this old red tractor for it?"

"I can help!"

"Perhaps," nodded Farmer Green. "The paint is still a bit chipped but I suppose I can do something about that."

"Yes," said Sally, "and I can help."

The morning of the rally was hot. Sally had polished the paint on the old red tractor so that it shone in the sunshine. She and Farmer Green drove it to where the rally was going to start.

There were all sorts of old tractors there, lined up along the side of the road. Farmer Green and Sally parked at the end of the line and went to collect a flag and a card with a number on it.

They tied the card onto the tractor and fixed on the flag. By the time the rally was due to start, there were about twenty tractors waiting to go. At the signal, they all started up.

They drove until lunch time, when all the tractors stopped and parked. They had a big picnic. Then everyone drove on to the finish line.

When Sally and Farmer Green arrived home that evening, they were worn out but happy. They parked the old red tractor back in the barn, and Sally gave it a quick polish to wipe off the dust from the road.

"I'm so glad you mended this tractor," she said. "I had a very good time."

I had such fun!

Farmer Green patted the tractor and smiled.

"Yes, so did I," he said, looking proudly at the prize in his hand. Not only had the old red tractor finished the whole rally, but it had got a prize for being the best-polished tractor of all!

What's in the book?

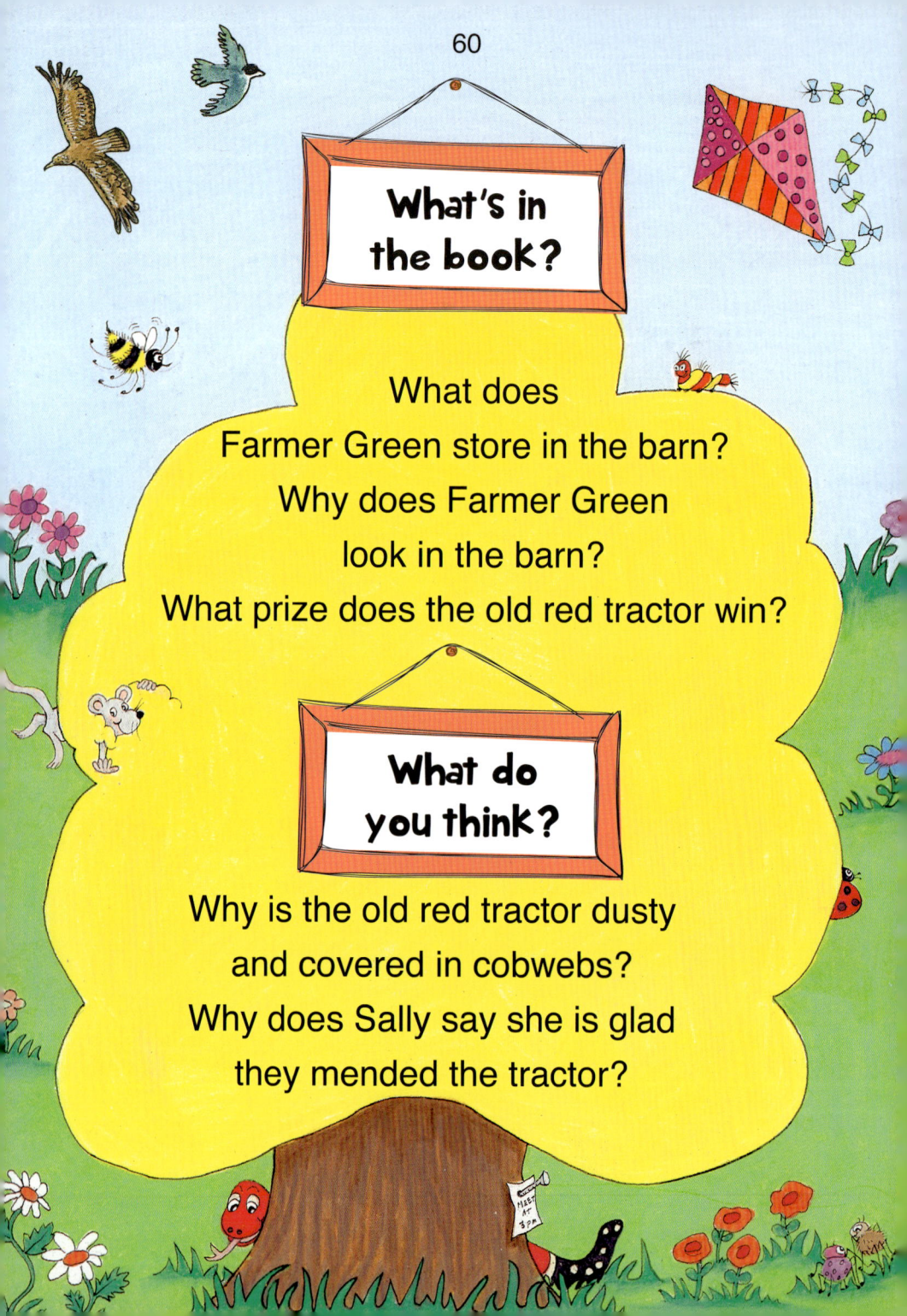

What does
Farmer Green store in the barn?
Why does Farmer Green
look in the barn?
What prize does the old red tractor win?

What do you think?

Why is the old red tractor dusty
and covered in cobwebs?
Why does Sally say she is glad
they mended the tractor?

The Model Boat

"Look at that boat!"

Zack and his Gramps liked to go down to the model boating lake, which was close to Gramps's house. In the summer, there were regattas on the lake. Lots of big model sailing boats took part in them. Zack had a little model boat, but it was too small to compete with the big ones.

Zack and Gramps wished they had a big sailing boat too. Gramps sent off for a kit as he was very good at building things.

"This bit is tricky!"

"Here is the sail."

When it arrived, Zack helped Gramps make a model sailing boat from the kit. It took them a long time.

The boat was made of plastic. She had tall sails with ribbon flags at the top and an extra set of sails for windy weather. They called her 'Jacamar'. Gramps made a stand for the boat's long keel, and they sat her on a shelf in his living room.

When she was completely finished, Gramps and Zack took Jacamar to the boating lake. They set her on the lake and off she sailed.

"She looks fantastic!" said Zack.
"Yes," Gramps agreed.

Zack ran around the lake and was just in time to stop Jacamar from crashing into the side. Then he sailed her back to Gramps. It was windy and there were quite big waves on the lake.

We did it!

Jacamar bobbed up and down.

Zack and Gramps sailed Jacamar back and forth across the lake. Suddenly, they spotted that she was starting to sink.

"You can do it!"

"Come on!" Zack begged the boat. "Sail a bit more. You can do it!" He stretched his arm out and tried his hardest to get hold of her.

But it was no good. Jacamar was just too far out on the lake.

"Help! She is sinking!" shouted Zack, starting to panic. Soon only the boat's flags were left sticking out of the lake. "Gramps!" he wailed miserably.

Gramps ran around the side of the boating lake to Zack. Without stopping to worry about his boots or trousers, he stepped into the lake and started to wade out.

It got deeper and deeper but Gramps kept going. As soon as he got to where the boat's flags were sticking up, he grabbed them.

He lifted up the boat and waved at Zack, who clapped and jumped about on the side of the lake. Gramps staggered back to give Zack the Jacamar.

"Got it!"

Zack took the boat and then helped Gramps out of the lake. Gramps was very wet and muddy.

"Thank you! I'm so glad you saved her!" cried Zack, giving Gramps a big hug.

Thank you!

Gramps gave Zack a wet smile.
"I think we had better go home," he said.

At home, Zack helped as Gramps dried himself off. Then they examined Jacamar together.

"She must have a hole in her somewhere," Gramps explained. They looked and looked for it until Gramps spotted a small metal pipe sticking out of the hull. "There!" he exclaimed. "We must have forgotten to fill that when we made her."

Gramps filled in the end of the little metal pipe.

"There we are, all finished!" he said, and smiled at Zack. "When that has dried, we can take her to the lake. She will not sink this time."

There we are!

Next weekend, Zack and Gramps went down to the boating lake again with Zack proudly carrying Jacamar.

"Look!"

There were lots of boats sailing on the lake, as there was going to be a regatta. Zack and Gramps hoped to take part this time.

Zack entered Jacamar in the regatta for children under ten. He set the sails and waited for the start.

CRACK! went the starter's pistol, and Zack let go of Jacamar.

She skimmed across the lake with the rest of the boats.

"Come on, come on, Jacamar!" Zack shouted, loudly.

He ran around to the far side of the lake to catch his boat. Then back across the lake she sailed.

"Come on, come on!" shouted Gramps. "You can do it! Come on, Zack!"

"Well," said Zack, at the end of the regatta. "We did not win, but I had a brilliant time. Can we bring Jacamar to the next regatta, too, Gramps?"

"Yes," smiled Gramps, "and perhaps next time we will win."

Zack and Gramps went home together, with Zack still proudly carrying Jacamar.

What's in the book?

What do Gramps and Zack make?
What happens when they sail Jacamar for the first time?
Do they win a prize?

What do you think?

What is a regatta?
Why does Zack give Gramps a big hug?

Wait and See!

One morning, a van stopped outside the house. A man got out, unloaded a big box, and wheeled it up to the house.

The big box was addressed to Jess and Zack's dad. It was as tall as Jess. She and Zack looked at it as it stood in the hall.

"Wait for your dad!"

"What is inside it?" said Zack.

"I suppose we will have to wait until Dad gets home," Jess replied.

Dad looked at the box as soon as he came home.

"Good," he said. "It has arrived."

"What has arrived?" cried Zack and Jess. "What is in the box?" But Dad just smiled again and said, "Wait and see."

He took the big box out to the shed and locked it up inside.

"It will be safe in there," he said.

"What will be safe in there?" said Zack.

"Wait and see!"

"Just let us have a quick look!" begged Jess. But Dad just smiled again and said, "Wait and see."

At the weekend, he spent a lot of time in the shed. Jess and Zack tried to see what he was doing. They offered to help him too, but it was no good.

"What can you see?"

"Why not?" cried Zack. Dad just smiled, maddeningly, and said, "Wait and see."

At dinner time, he came out of the shed and locked it.

"Did you make something?" said Zack, as Dad came in. "Is it finished yet?"

"Wait and see!"

"And can we see it?" Jess added.

"No, not yet," said Dad. "You can wait and see." He smiled at them.

Zack and Jess tried to peek into the shed, but it was too dark for them to see what was inside.

"What can it be?" said Zack.

"It was a big box," Jess pointed out.

"It was tall but flat," said Zack. "It must be something Dad has to make, as he took it to the shed. But I cannot guess what it is."

So Zack and Jess just had to wait. Dad continued to smile and to tell them to wait and see. At the weekends, he spent a lot of time in the shed, hammering and painting.

Splosh!

Bang!

Bang!

Tap!

Tap!

Then, one morning, Dad came out of the shed and into the kitchen.

"Guess what!" he said. "I have finished!"

"Finished what?" said Zack.

"I bet we still have to wait and see," said Jess.

"Not this time," said Dad, proudly. "Come and look!"

Zack and Jess did not wait to be told again. They jumped up and rushed outside.

By the shed, Dad stopped and smiled down at Jess.

"This is for you, Jess," he said to her.

"For me?" said Jess, and Dad nodded. He took them into the shed to see what he had made.

Let's go in!

There, inside on the bench, was a little house.

"Thank you, Dad!" exclaimed Jess. "Is it for dolls?"

Thank you!

Dad nodded.

"It is a bit like the one that Jess liked so much when we visited that big old house," said Zack.

"Yes," said Dad. "That is why I made her this one as a present."

Jess and Zack looked at the house. It was painted lavender, with dark stones down the sides. There were tiles on the roof, and inside there were six big rooms.

"All the rooms are painted white," said Zack.

"Yes," Dad agreed. "Jess will have to help me decorate them. She can pick out the paints herself."

"This is like my bedroom, and that is like Zack's," said Jess, pointing to the rooms at the top of the house. "I am going to make them look just like our bedrooms."

"You will need to get a very small bunk bed for your one, then," said Zack, "with lots of little fluffy animals to go on it." Then he grinned. "Do they make small toilets?" he chuckled.

Jess helped Dad to paint all the rooms inside the house. They found some old bits of carpet that they cut down to size. When they had finished painting it, Dad helped Jess take the little house into her bedroom.

It looks good!

Jess spent a long time sitting and looking at her house, thinking about it.

"I will have to start collecting things to go in it," she said to herself. It was going to be fun choosing all the things to go inside. "Perhaps I can make some little quilts to go on the beds," she said aloud to Rags.

Just then, Zack came in. He was carrying a small box.

"Dad said to give you this," he said. Jess took the lid off the box. There inside it was a family of little dolls.

"They are exactly what I need to live in my house!" cried Jess happily.

What's in the book?

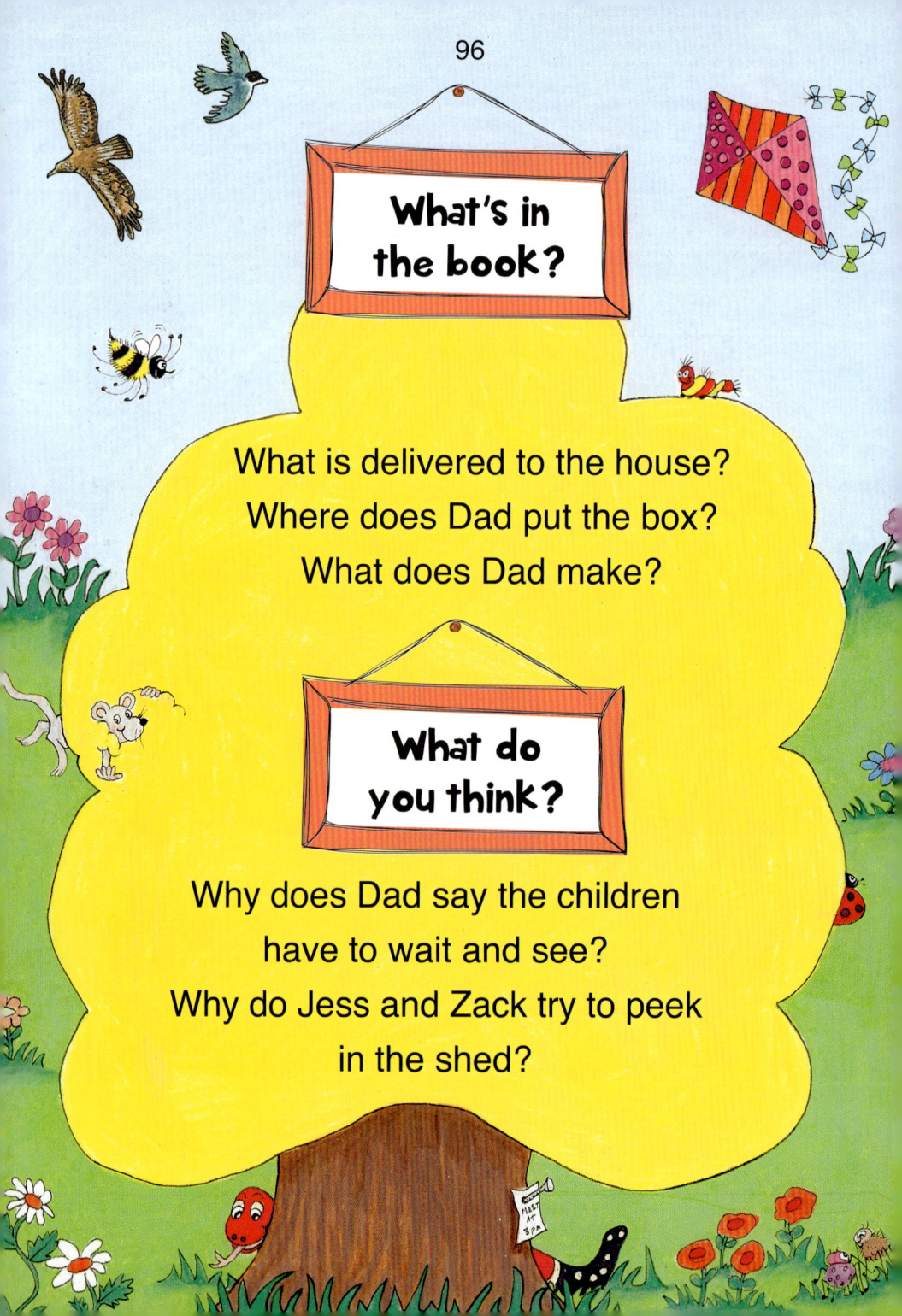

What is delivered to the house?
Where does Dad put the box?
What does Dad make?

What do you think?

Why does Dad say the children have to wait and see?
Why do Jess and Zack try to peek in the shed?

The Bad-Tempered Goat

Farmer Green had lots of animals on his farm. Besides the cats – Molly and Tolly – and the sheepdogs – Ben and Neb – there were sheep, pigs, rabbits, hens and one old billy goat.

The goat had a very bad temper. He snorted and shouted loudly when he was angry. Sometimes, he got so angry that he ran into things and butted them with his horns.

Snort!

One morning, Farmer Green was feeding the animals in the yard. He had milk for the cats, bones for the dogs, corn for the hens, carrots for the rabbits and a sack of oats for the goat.

"Good morning!" called Farmer Green, as he tipped the sack into the bucket in the goat's shed. The goat replied with a snort and ran to make a start on his oats. He had a big appetite, and he was very hungry.

Snort!

Suddenly, a cheeky little robin swooped down and snatched up some of the oats. Then she fluttered up into an oak tree and sat down to finish up the oats.

Snort!

The bad-tempered goat looked up at the robin in amazement.

"Good morning," the little robin sang down to him. "These are very fine oats you have."

Snort!

The goat snorted angrily and stamped his hooves. Then he shook his head in disgust and bent down to have some oats.

When she had finished her oats, the cheeky little robin came down from the tree for more. She fluttered down, landing on one of the goat's horns!

This was too much for the bad-tempered goat, who got extremely angry. He ran up and down alongside the wall, snorting and stamping his hooves.

Moo!

Stamp!

Then he stopped and looked up, expecting to see that the robin had gone. Instead, there she was, looking cheekily down at him from the oak tree.

The goat stamped his hooves, bent his head and started to run at the tree. He was glad to see that this time the robin fled in alarm. He butted the tree trunk hard with his horns, and there was a loud CRUNCH as they smashed into it.

CRUNCH!

The tree groaned and shook, and then, with a SNAP, CRACK, CRASH, it came tumbling down on top of the goat, who found himself trapped under it.

"Help!"

"Help!" he cried. "Help!"

"This is heavy!"

"Get me out!"

Farmer Green came running to see what all the noise was about. On seeing that the goat was stuck, he rushed to help, but the tree was too heavy for him to lift up by himself.

"I need the old red tractor!" he shouted, running off to get it. He soon drove back in it and parked it by the fallen tree. Then he ran off again to fetch a rope.

When he got back, he tied one end of the rope around the tree trunk and one end to a hook at the back of the tractor.

Farmer Green started up the tractor and used it to drag the tree along the ground, until it was off the goat completely. Then he stopped the tractor, jumped down and ran back to have a look. The goat was free, but he did not get up.

I will call the vet

"I think I had better call Eric, the vet," said Farmer Green.

When Eric arrived, he felt the goat's legs and ribs up and down. Then he and Farmer Green helped the goat to stand up.

There, there.

Keep still.

The goat was feeling a bit silly, and he waited while Eric checked him one more time, without stamping, snorting or shouting.

"The goat has been very lucky," explained Eric. "He is a bit stunned, but he will be fine in a little while. Perhaps this will stop him being so bad-tempered next time," he added, patting the goat on the head.

The goat, who had started to feel a bit better, looked up at Eric and snorted as grumpily as ever. Eric looked at Farmer Green and broke into a grin.

Ha! Ha! Ha!

Snort!

"Then again, perhaps not!" he said. Farmer Green just shook his head and smiled.

What's in the book?

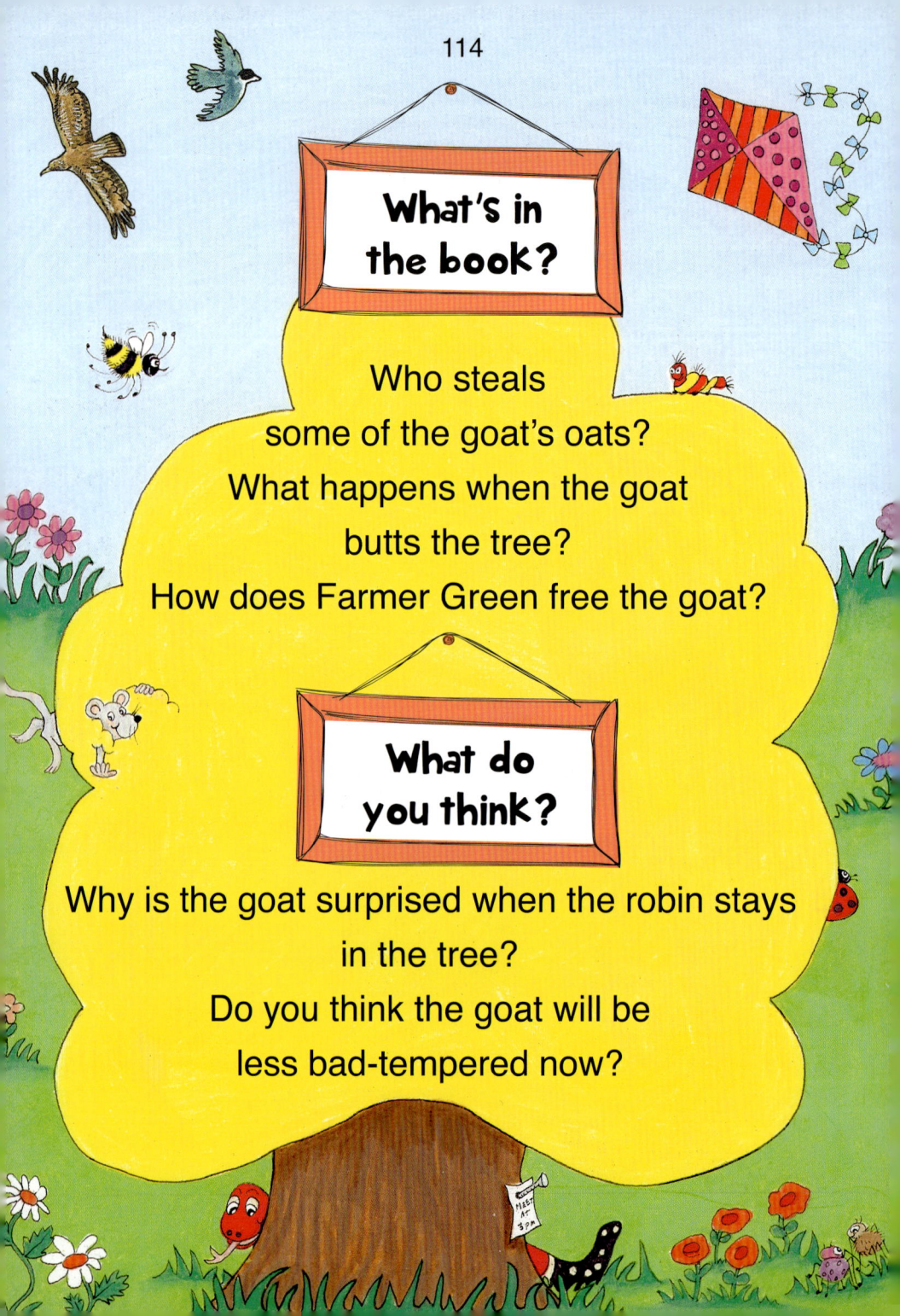

Who steals some of the goat's oats?
What happens when the goat butts the tree?
How does Farmer Green free the goat?

What do you think?

Why is the goat surprised when the robin stays in the tree?
Do you think the goat will be less bad-tempered now?

Parents

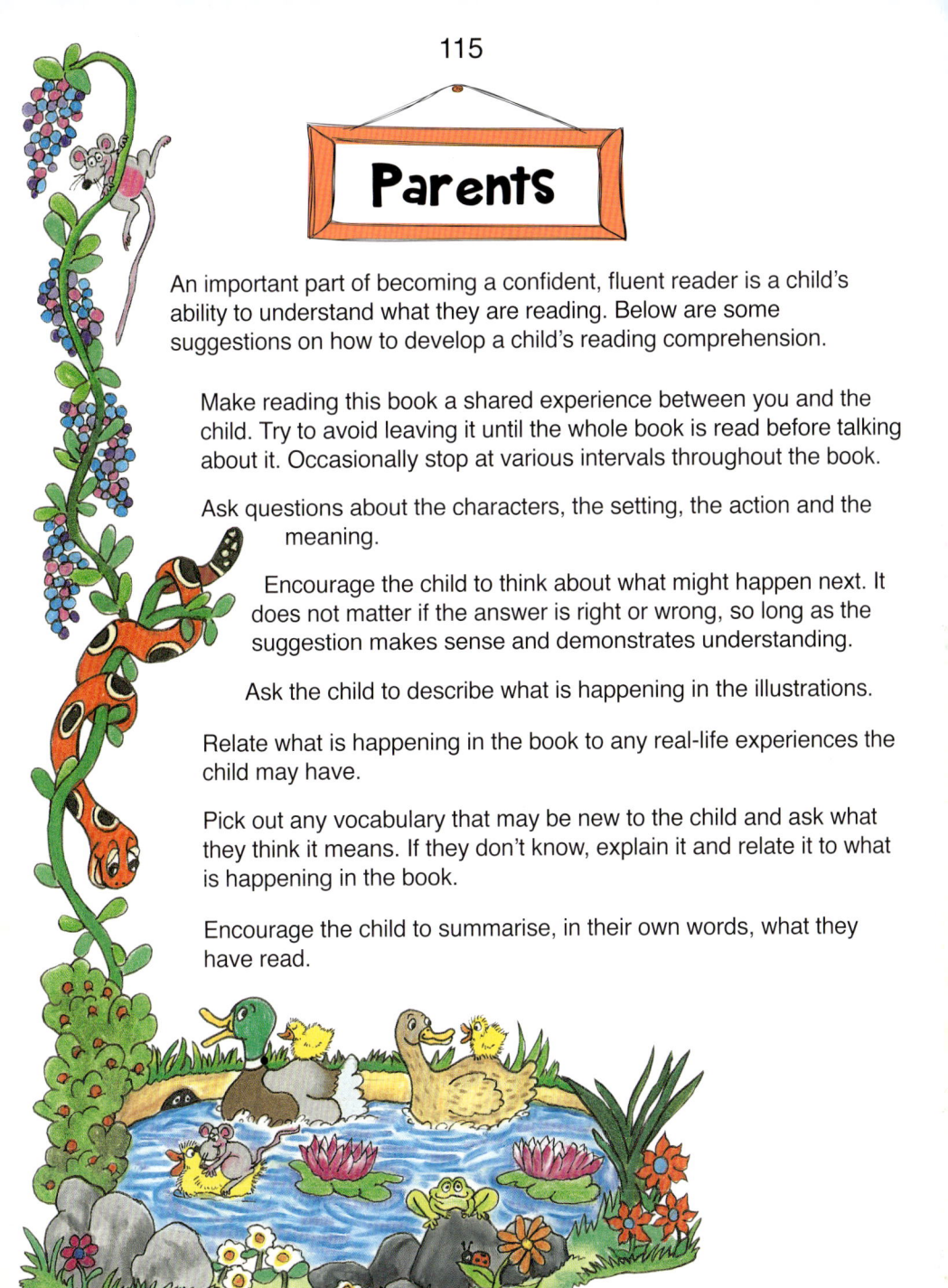

An important part of becoming a confident, fluent reader is a child's ability to understand what they are reading. Below are some suggestions on how to develop a child's reading comprehension.

Make reading this book a shared experience between you and the child. Try to avoid leaving it until the whole book is read before talking about it. Occasionally stop at various intervals throughout the book.

Ask questions about the characters, the setting, the action and the meaning.

Encourage the child to think about what might happen next. It does not matter if the answer is right or wrong, so long as the suggestion makes sense and demonstrates understanding.

Ask the child to describe what is happening in the illustrations.

Relate what is happening in the book to any real-life experiences the child may have.

Pick out any vocabulary that may be new to the child and ask what they think it means. If they don't know, explain it and relate it to what is happening in the book.

Encourage the child to summarise, in their own words, what they have read.

Book Review

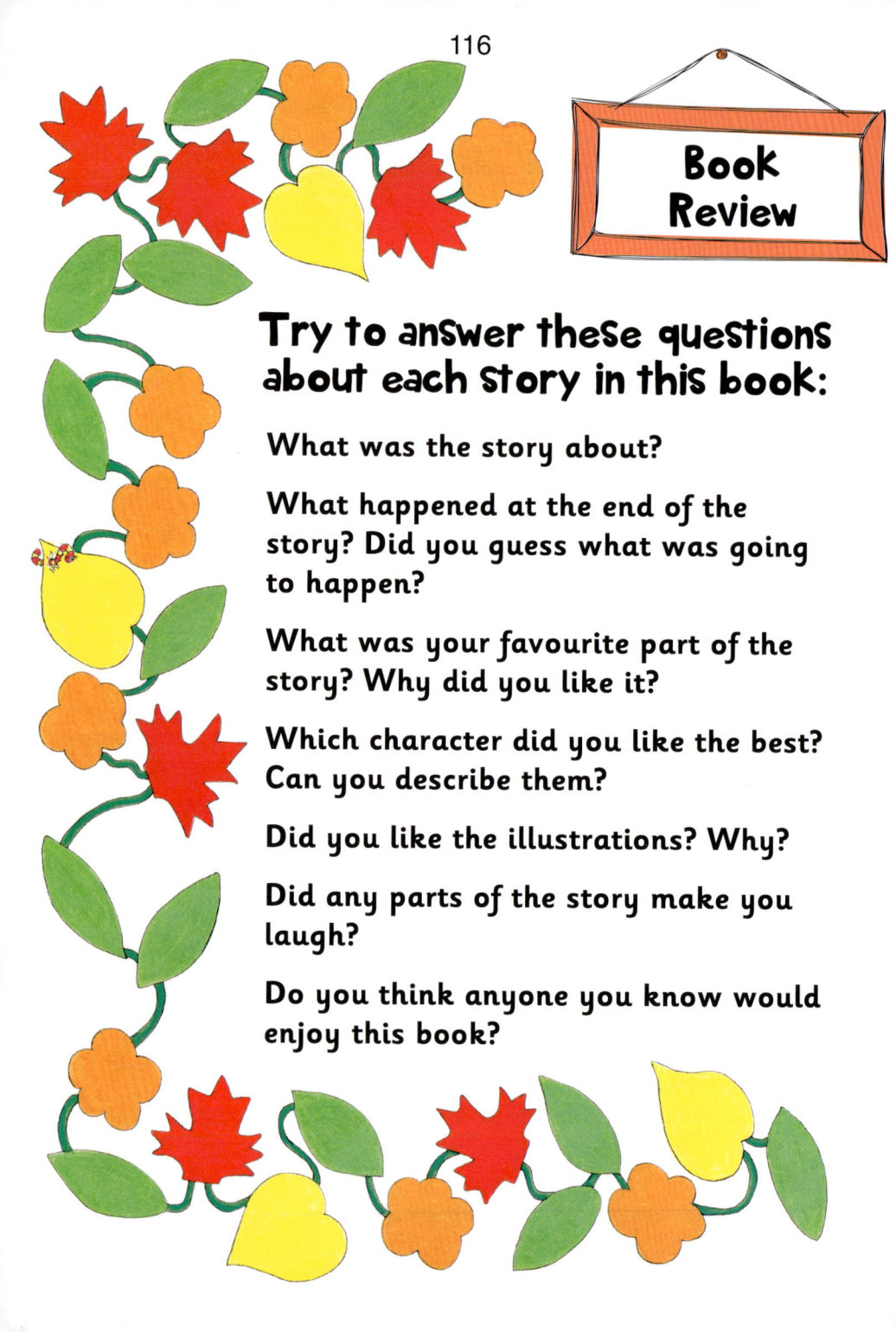

Try to answer these questions about each story in this book:

What was the story about?

What happened at the end of the story? Did you guess what was going to happen?

What was your favourite part of the story? Why did you like it?

Which character did you like the best? Can you describe them?

Did you like the illustrations? Why?

Did any parts of the story make you laugh?

Do you think anyone you know would enjoy this book?

Could you re-tell the story in your own words?

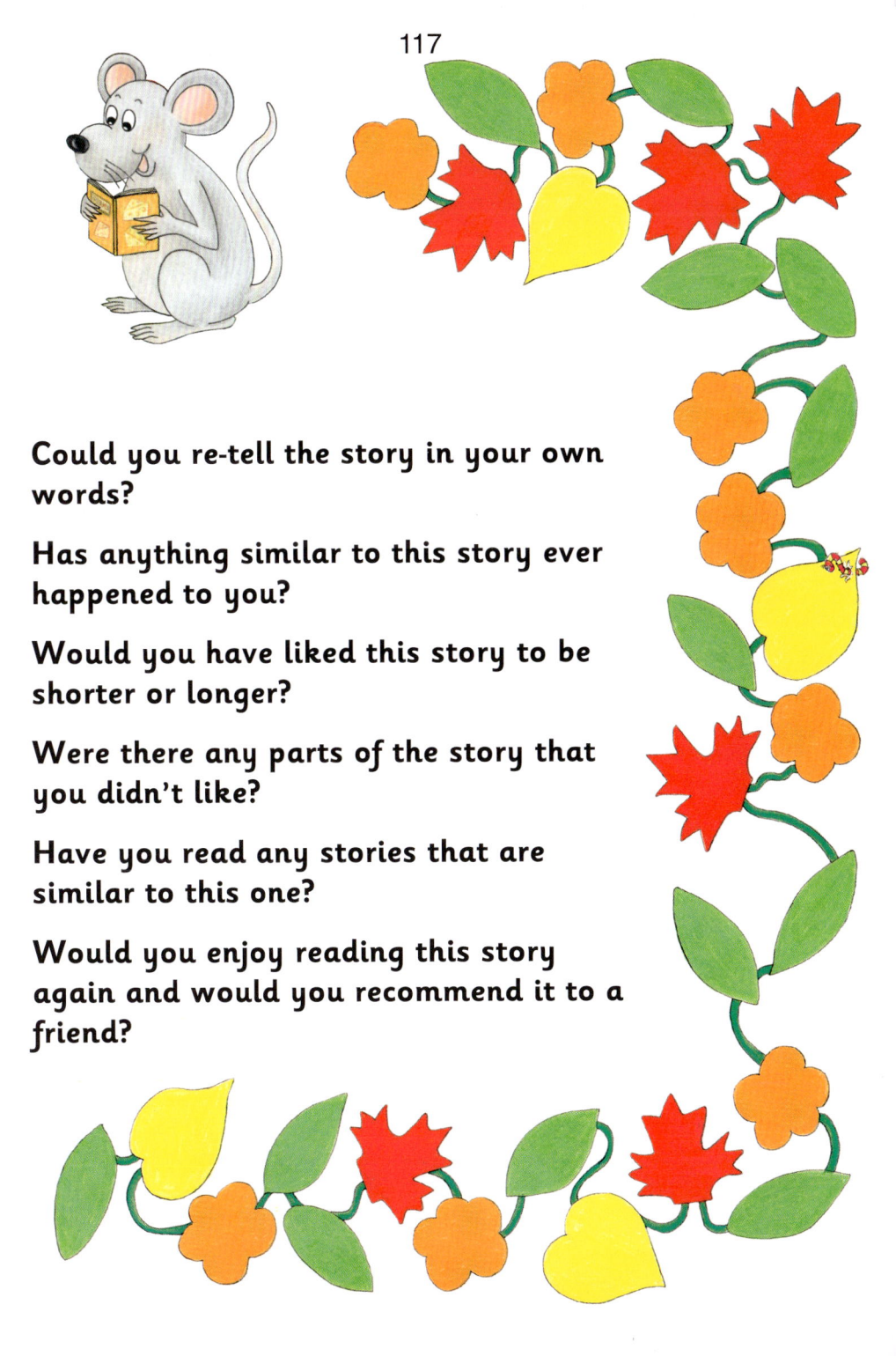

Has anything similar to this story ever happened to you?

Would you have liked this story to be shorter or longer?

Were there any parts of the story that you didn't like?

Have you read any stories that are similar to this one?

Would you enjoy reading this story again and would you recommend it to a friend?

Character Review

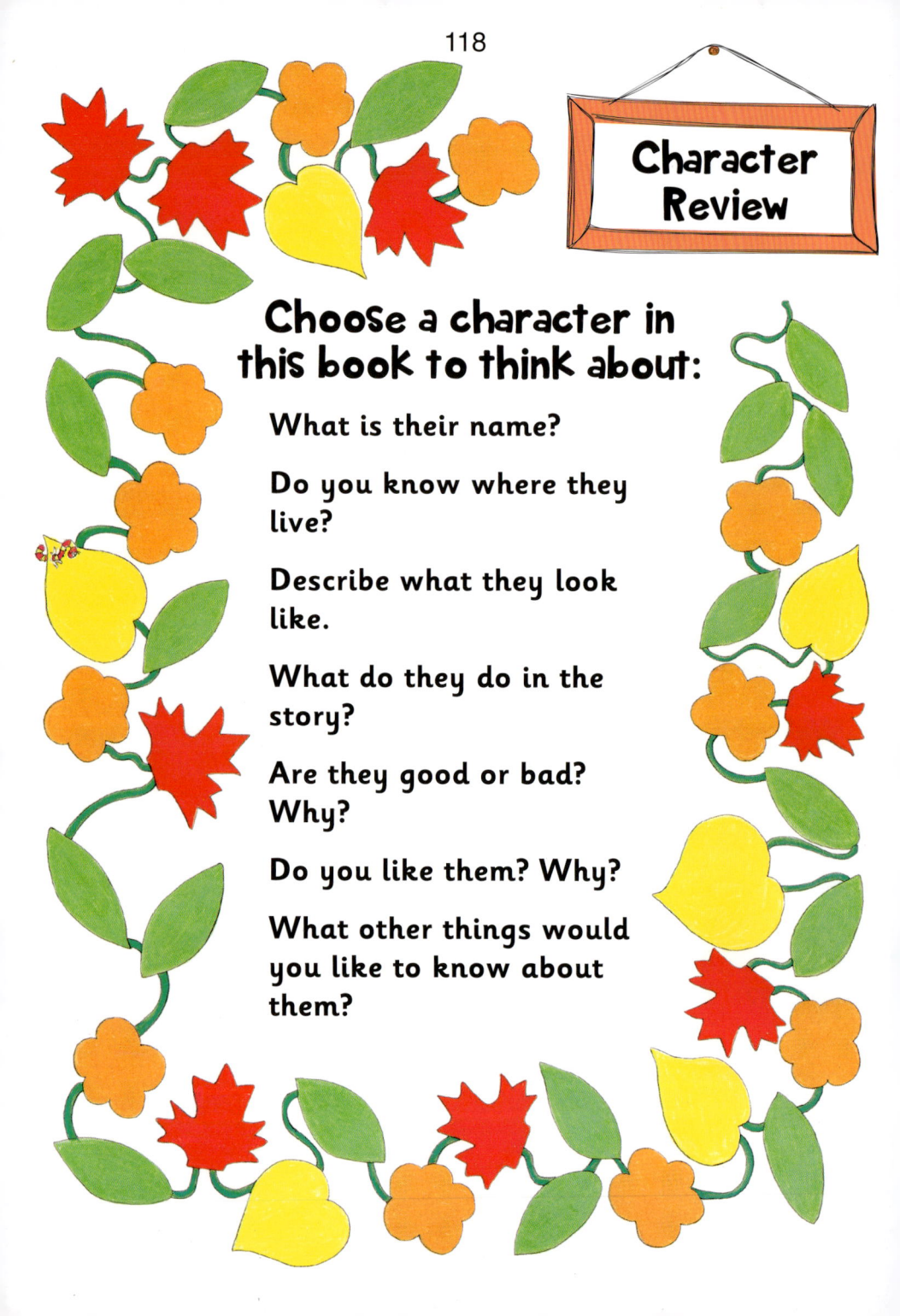

Choose a character in this book to think about:

What is their name?

Do you know where they live?

Describe what they look like.

What do they do in the story?

Are they good or bad? Why?

Do you like them? Why?

What other things would you like to know about them?